Phoenix

Transformation Poems

Phoenix

Transformation Poems

by Jessica Goody

CW Books

© 2019 by Jessica Goody

Published by CW Books
P.O. Box 541106
Cincinnati, OH 45254-1106

ISBN: 9781625493064

Poetry Editor: Kevin Walzer
Business Editor: Lori Jareo

Visit us on the web at www.readcwbooks.com

To my grandmother
with love and gratitude.

Thank you for everything.

I am eternally grateful for the love, support, guidance, and friendship of the people in my life, especially Marjorie, Chrystie, and Jacqueline Goody; Seabert, Maiya and Coco; Brendan, Lee and Maureen Jolley; the Benyaminy family, Cora Burkhardt, Fern Schwartz and Mike Kinsella, David Goldstein, Raymond Brunjes, and Dr. Hylton Lightman; Sue Howell, David Graham, Linda and Hubie Coleman, Jerri Hanna, Jim Brunner, Will Ross, Rita Ross, Carl and Lara Hausler, Donna McCann; the members of the Sun City SunScribers, especially Carol Hixson, Hal Meeks, Carla Bech-Hansen, Frank Cinami, Jack Callender, Chris Roosa, Brian Thiem, Audrey Friedman, Janet Docherty and Adele Winney; Roscoe and Midge Sandlin, Jan Henson Dow, Phil Tannenholz, Karl and Judy Barons, Ed Phelps, Mary Kay Montgomery, Larry and Carol Della Vecchia, Robert McCloskey, Edward Galloway, Bob Taylor, Gwyneth Saunders, Joanne Murray, Wendell and Bernadette MacNeal; Dr. Ellen Malphrus, Don McCauley of *The Authors Show*, Bonnie Blose of Behind Our Eyes, Rockelle Henderson and the Bluffton Book Festival, Elizabeth Robin, the Island Writers Network, Jacquelyn Markham and the members of Otram Slabess; Jack Gannon, Cyndi Barnier-Williams, and Authors Under the Live Oaks, Wanda Jerideau, Valerie Dunn, Kim Poovey, Laurie McCall, Stephanie Austin Edwards, Kimberly Wilson, Andrea Scher, Lynda McKinney Lambert, Libby Ricardo, Carrie and Tyrel Faires, Lois Kazenski, Cindy Bricker, Andrea Sisino, and Jim Nicholson of the Osher Lifelong Learning Institute; Carol Weir and *The Hilton Head Monthly*, and Christopher Dow of Phosphene Publishing.

I gratefully acknowledge the editors of the publications in which versions of many of these poems first appeared: Dustin D.

Pickering of *Harbinger Asylum* and Transcendent Zero Press, Cate Fitzpatrick of *The Island Packet*, Davon Loeb of Connotation Press, Kae Sable of *The Dime Show Review*, Jim Finnegan of *The Wallace Stevens Journal*, David Jibson and Joe Ferrari of *Third Wednesday*, Anthony Costello of *The High Window*, Lynne Hummell of *The Bluffton Sun*, Charles E. J. Moulton of *The Creativity Webzine*, Mary Jo Lord of *Magnets and Ladders*, Gordon Krupsky of *The MacGuffin*, James Browning Kepple of *The Kitchen Poet*, N. I. Nicholson of *Barking Sycamores*, Michael Northen of *Wordgathering* and the Disability Literature Consortium, Nick Hale and James P. Wagner of Local Gems Poetry Press\Bards Initiative, Helen Bar-Lev and JohnMichael Simon of Cyclamens and Swords Publishing, Eve Hanninen of *The Centifugal Eye*, and Onkar Sharma of *The Literary Yard*.

I am particularly grateful to Marjorie Goody, Harvey Trabb, Miho Kinnas, and Olivia Stiffler, who acted as beta readers for this poetry manuscript, generously offering their time, advice and enthusiasm.

Acknowledgements

"Another Storm" previously appeared in *Harbinger Asylum*.

"Backstage" previously appeared in *The Creativity Webzine* and *Cyclamens and Swords*.

"Bitter Tea" previously appeared in *The Kitchen Poet* and the anthology *Bards Annual 2016*.

"Blue Landscape" previously appeared in *Third Wednesday* and *The Creativity Webzine*.

"Blue Rhapsody" previously appeared in *The Creativity Webzine*.

"Bruegel's Bride" previously appeared in *The MacGuffin* and *The Centrifugal Eye*.

"Casa Azul" previously appeared in *The Creativity Webzine*, *Barking Sycamores*, and the anthology *Barking Sycamores: Year Two*.

"The Color of Moonlight" previously appeared in *Cyclamens and Swords*.

"Discoveries" previously appeared in *The Dime Show Review*, *The Creativity Webzine*, and the anthology *Bards Annual 2017*.

"Images" previously appeared in *Harbinger Asylum*.

"Jazz" previously appeared in *The Creativity Webzine* and *The Centrifugal Eye*.

"Madonna and Child" previously appeared in *The Creativity Webzine* and the anthology *Inspired By My Museum*.

"Memory" previously appeared in *Cyclamens and Swords*.

"Mona Lisa" previously appeared in *Third Wednesday*.

"The Moon Stalker" previously appeared in *Harbinger Asylum*.

"Nerves" previously appeared in *Magnets and Ladders* and *The Creativity Webzine*.

"Northern Lights" previously appeared in *Harbinger Asylum*.

"Ode to Katharine Hepburn" previously appeared in *The Creativity Webzine*, *Barking Sycamores* and their anthology *Barking Sycamores: Year Two*.

"Portrait in Green" previously appeared in *Magnets and Ladders* and *The Creativity Webzine*.

"Potatoes" previously appeared in *The High Window*, *The Creativity Webzine*, and *The Kitchen Poet*.

"Rehearsal" previously appeared in *The Creativity Webzine*.

"Revelation" previously appeared in *Harbinger Asylum*.

"Reverie" previously appeared in *Cyclamens and Swords*.

"Spirituality" previously appeared in *The Creativity Webzine*.

"Summer Fruit" previously appeared in *The Kitchen Poet*, *Cyclamens and Swords*, and *The Creativity Webzine*.

"Words" previously appeared in *The Literary Yard*.

"Words and Music" previously appeared in *The Creativity Webzine*.

Table of Contents

Jazz	17
Bitter Tea	19
Revelation	22
Dusk	23
After Sunset	24
Changeling	25
The Color of Moonlight	26
Reflections	27
Scenes from A Kimono	29
Tsukimi	31
Morning Tea	32
The Moon Stalker	33
Tigers	34
Foraging	35
Portrait in Green	36
Blue Landscape	37
Discoveries	38
The Edge of the World	39
Excavation	40
Memory	41
Reverie	42
Prague	43
Heirlooms	44
Miranda	45
Stardust	47
Desire	48
Another Storm	49
Nerves	50
Images	51
Spirituality	52
Backstage	53
Rehearsal	54
Blue Rhapsody	55
Silent Sentinels	56

Ode to Katharine Hepburn	57
Cat Eyes	58
The Crimson Rug	59
Madonna and Child	60
Painting Mary Magdalene	61
Bruegel's Bride	62
Mona Lisa	64
Posing for Renoir	65
Casa Azul	66
Greenwich Village	67
Along the Amazon	68
Green Shadows	69
Waltz of the Hawks	70
Wetlands	71
Landscape	72
The Gathering Storm	73
Reconstruction	74
Fallen Leaves	75
Death in Autumn	76
Sacred Trees	77
The Guise of the Phoenix	78
Between Pacific Tides	79
Tarpon River, Fort Lauderdale	80
Northern Lights	81
Evil Stars	82
Runestones	83
Words	84
Irises	86
Spring Rain	87
Words and Music	88
The Front Page	89
Skin	90
Summer Fruit	91
Tahitian Landscape	92
Potatoes	93

Soul Song..95

About the Author...97

Jazz

Inspired by the work of Henri Matisse

Patterns catch the eye, crawling along wallpaper and
upholstery in a melange of colors and textures, rendering
the room as exotic as a harem, draped with vivid
slipcovers of Moroccan arabesques and damasks.

The wallpaper blooms humid tropical foliage,
blood-red blossoms unfurling behind the heads
of odalisques reclining on striped pillows, the divan
curving beneath them like the body of a lover.

A backdrop of vibrant fabrics curtain the room like a seraglio.
Oushaks and kilims burn underfoot as the light shines
through the lacework windows and shuttered doors,
where beaded lamps drip crystals atop runner-draped tables.

Orchids and potted plants crowd every surface, swarming
the carved mantel and bowlegged iron tables. Lovingly
arranged, the palm fronds spread their graceful green arms
to the sun, tendrils inching upwards like ivy.

Joyful nudes dance along the walls. Cobalt blue outlines
like police silhouettes stretch and tumble, leap and caper.

Tinted ultramarine, the color of distant horizons,
they resemble woad-stained Celts, rangy of limb and sinew.

Matisse lies abed in his atelier, industrious as Proust,
surrounded by a sea of colored paper, scattered leaves
and whimsical shapes that might be flowers or flames,
strewn petals drifting to the floor like shards of glass.

Bitter Tea

The tea was bitter with betrayal.
Their knowing eyes met across the table
among the sugar tongs and strawberries.
Blackflies lingered over the sugar cubes,
waved away by impatient hands.

The spoons rang against the teacups with
a chime like church bells. The ice clatters,
catching light like glaciers in a sepia sea,
melting fast under the steady eye of the sun.
The rising steam unfurls to meet the sky,

evaporating like a jet's contrail overhead,
its warm scent drifting against perfumes.
Smiling over sandwiches, his wife stirs angrily,
Her jaw strained taut with furious hostility.
The teasing frisson of electricity leapt

between their mingled fingertips. Concealed
beneath the tablecloth, She tickled his ankles
with her painted toes, her sandals abandoned
in the grass. A cool green afternoon awash with
light, drifting tendrils of windblown hair and

laughter like wind chimes, bone china gleaming

against her vermillion fingertips. The strawberries
bleed against the porcelain. The world is green and
expectant. The leaves shiver in the breeze, throwing
shadows on stippled bark. The fresh-peach scent of

the bower sweet as the summer nectar of sweat-damp
sheets, a strand of hair stark against the pristine pillow.
Her legs are crossed decorously beneath the whiteness
of the napkin stained with the blown kiss of Her lipstick.
The sunlight illuminates her shape through the voile

of Her summer dress like stained glass, lit from within.
He lingers in the curve of Her neck, kissing its white
softness and murmuring in Her ear. They whisper into
the wind, stealing secret moments of breathless
conversation, finger-painting their linked initials on the

sweating glasses and smearing them clean. The civility
of convention, the pouring of the steaming pot, leaves
unfurling. The crystal click of ice cubes clattering in
the topaz tea, sugar swirling like sand, the sharpness
of citrus filling the air. The long spoons catch the light,

winking at their duplicity. His wife worries the teabag with
a spoon, watching the water darken. The broken shards
of their relationship cannot be repaired with decorum
and cups of tea, pallid weapons against the calculating
sensuality of Her smile, as ripe and overt as summer fruit.

Revelation

Inspired by W. B. Yeats

I am swollen with your own potential,
teetering on a precipice over the sea.
While I wait, the moon ticks toward retrograde.
When the last grain of sand clears the hourglass,

you will lose me, the child-melon of my stomach
rising like a red balloon, a dream on a string.
She will tear you apart and pick your bones clean.
Later, will you climb upstairs in the dark,

desolate and seeking sympathy,
a single, symbolic candle throwing shadows
on the wall, and come to me, an afterthought?
The clandestine moon might have an answer.

I could consult the cards, the ghosts,
my moon-belly smooth and swollen as new fruit.

Dusk

The fading sphere of the setting sun
resembles a blood orange,
the juice being squeezed from the fruit.

Golden light streaks the rug
with the mellow hush of sunset,
warmth making a final stand

before the dying of the day.
The ebbing light glows through the blinds
like a half-lidded eye watching the sunset unfurl.

After Sunset

A single lamppost,
stark and attenuated,
glows against the dark.

Changeling

I knew it in the cold North Sea
of my subconscious, where the wave
of marrow-deep truth burst onto shore.

I can remember the sound of your laughter,
the candles burning blue like your eyes.
Now the candles burn low with impatience,

and the telephone sits white and forgotten
where you no longer call,
countries and waters away from where I sit.

I wait to the hold music of remembered conversations
without your shadow, your scent,
the curve of your smile to guide me.

The Color of Moonlight

A boudoir strewn with silk pajamas and lingerie,
a white embroidered kimono draped on a chair,
A tufted headboard rising over supple sheets of
creamy linen, pristinely pale, scattered with satin

throw pillows. The gossamer drapes are the color
of moonlight. Silk scarves spread like butterfly wings
on an antique bureau with a fluted mirror, bearing
a silver vanity set, delicately etched; cut-glass flagons,

tortoiseshell combs, and the scent of powder in the air,
like the barefoot sensuality of a sheepskin rug on a
sunlit floor, or the tawny prowl of an amber-eyed cat.
A string of pearls, a cool strand of miniature moons,

gleaming among the silver squares of picture frames.
Vanilla tapers flicker in crystal candlesticks, adding
their scent to the sweetly-spreading petals of bouquets:
drooping heads of calla lilies, the pale spirals of roses

in a porcelain vase resting on the carved white mantel.
A velvet sofa curved like a sleeping woman, sprawling
supine and sleek, draped in leopard lushness among
inlaid tables, rich woods polished to a palomino gloss.

Reflections

On the bygone dressing table sits a row
of cut-glass bottles now bereft of perfume.
They say that scent stirs the memory.

I lift the crystal stopper, but no ancient aroma
wafts from the vial to resurrect the past.
The old vanity is scattered with notions and toiletries:

a sachet, its musk vanished with age, herbs and leaves
the color of old paper, and crushed to powder.
In the mirror, a long-forgotten lady appears before me.

A locket, gold mellowed to brassiness, a cameo,
the tiny silhouette smiling in carved bas-relief.
A lace handkerchief, its embroidered monogram

 as precise and elegant as calligraphy.
A powder puff, a silver hand mirror,
heavy as cast-iron, hair combs;

a silver butterfly poised in flight,
its iridescent wings made of abalone.
A needlepoint reticule blooming with roses

and a folded fan, to be snapped coyly at admirers.
rapier hatpins lie scattered on the silver tray, steely
needles capped with crystals like twinkling stars.

Scenes from A Kimono

I

Shining dragons creep
from gilded pagodas, scales
etched, talons curling.

II

Plumes of rising smoke
twist and swirl into contrails,
eyes yellow and cold.

III

Forked tongues are singed by
rainbow flames of burning breath.
Catfish sashay past.

IV

Koi flash like sunsets.
Golden threads of fishing lures

glint against blue silk.

V

The red blossom of
of lips, hair impaled in shining
origami folds.

Tsukimi

I

Yellow leaves drift down
like feathers, the generous
currency of trees.

II

The moon is swollen
like a grin, delighting in
her golden secrets.

III

Bathing in her glow,
scattered stars flicker and flirt,
clinging close as curves.

Morning Tea

The kettle hisses
like the cicadas outside
the kitchen window.

The Moon Stalker

I

Tigers stalk the night,
prowling in the green darkness,
glowing like the moon.

II

A golden surprise,
their eyes flash in the shadows,
striped with smoke and flame.

Tigers

I have been plundered by tigers.
They reclaim their lost heritage:
The lush play of muscle against fur,
ivory ripped from once-fierce jaws,

the burning pelt torn from
the xylophone of vertebrae,
bare bones pale and opalescent,
tossed aside like careless dice.

A throaty crescendo builds
in the air like a gathering storm.
Their eyes flash in the shadows,
glowing like the waxing moon.

Foraging

Elephants move through
the darkness like smoke, stamping
the well-trodden grass

of the savannah,
a sere expanse unsoftened
by mystical trees.

Mountainous shadows,
skin wrinkled like fingerprints,
grey against the green.

Portrait in Green

Inspired by Barbara Kingsolver's *The Poisonwood Bible*

The mamba is green as new leaves.
A lion follows, stealthy as a spy
in his pursuit of me, a lame gazelle.

Mirror-image palindromes
flash in my bloodless brain,
revealing asymmetrical secrets.

Spiderwebs like woven gauze curtain
ancient sprawling baobabs, gnarled
spreading roots parched in the Equatorial heat.

The kiss of the green snake leaves you frozen,
twin pinpricks on your arm like vampire fangs.
The jungle spreads its skirts in a thousand shades of green.

I trudge through red dust, my heavy tread distinct
in the green silence: the slap and thud of my dragging feet.

Blue Landscape

(Marc Chagall, "Couple in a Blue Landscape", 1949)

They lie in the curve of the crescent moon,
a cosmic cradle, a gondola hovering in the sky.
He admires her lapis hair, her bare shoulders

and sodalite skin. A thousand shades of blue flicker,
rendering them luminous and ethereal as mermaids,
blue-green women with bodies as ripe as dark plums.

Floating in a cerulean spotlight, her bare toes pearly
and stricken blue, she strokes his hair, whispering of
the secret world swelling in her stomach. Her bare belly

echoes the curve of the moon, a swallowed pearl.
Seraphim twirl in the richness of a cobalt sky, swooping
and diving like silent, moonstruck birds. Missile-shaped

fish swim in the depths where elemental spirits swirl and
crest like waves. Mythological beasts stalk this enchanted
forest gone as blue-green as the flame in an emerald's eye.

Discoveries

Inspired by the photography of Frank Hurley during the
Shackleton Imperial Trans-Antarctic Expedition, 1914

Imagine a cold of frightening intensity,
a region defined by lack of temperature.
Islets rise like moles on the expanse of

the silver-nitrate sea, glaciers shaped like plateaus,
fortresses, mountain ranges. Palaces of ice drift by,
flashing colors in the sun. Inside, mottled maps

paper the walls, a spiderweb of constellations
to steer by. Snowshoes latticed with rawhide,
and specimen trays of stones and shells

preserved in the icebox of the Arctic.
Heavy trunks with handsome brass
fittings, their elegance now tarnished.

Inside, abandoned flotsam lies perfectly preserved:
tin cans and melted stalks of candles, the hulk of
an antique typewriter, and an elegant gramophone,

its gleaming horn fluted like a seashell. One hundred
years ago, it played Strauss to a curious audience
of penguins who had never heard music before.

The Edge of the World

The sheer space is vast and magnificent,
intimidating in its scope. Standing on the
divide between frozen serenity and howling
wilderness, I feel the lives of the intrepid

behind me, their icy breath whipping my
hair as the wind whips my face. The world
is whitewashed, gleaming, calm and holy.
Elements compete in brightness: glaciers,

stars and churning waves mirroring shafts
of light. I stand here, observing this place
of contradictions, paradoxes, extremes:
Deep silence filled with the tones of icy

winds and animal calls; light so pure
and clear, rich with everything of life.

Excavation

"Full fathom five thy father lies;
Of his bones are coral made;
Those are pearls that were his eyes:
Nothing of him that doth fade
But doth suffer a sea-change
Into something rich and strange."

-William Shakespeare, *The Tempest*

Columns of bones stand tall as floor lamps, thick as barbells.
Their knobbed femurs are tipped with gemstones like finials.
Ancient periwinkles stained the violet of imperial robes, and

stones etched with prehistoric runes gouged by tooth and claw.
An ammonite, inlaid and glittering, ringed with traces of blue,
casts rainbows like flickering foil, enchanted, magical, unreal.

The crescent-curve of claw glows green as if lit by radiation.
Opalescent bones and teeth striped with turquoise and cobalt,
neon-lit in impossible colors that resemble flashing fish.

Broken shards are dappled the blue-green-violet of the
aurora borealis, fragments gleaming chrysoprase, lapis,
aquamarine; indigo spears the burning blue of methane.

Memory

Everything he loves about her is gone.
Her face is frozen, blank as new paper,
once-dark eyebrows faded to whiteness.
Her mouth drags now, the pinpricks of

dimples no longer flickering in the curve
of her cheek. Her skin is slack and creased
with wrinkles, the joints stiff and swollen.
Her long fingers gnarled and crone-cold,

legs etched with blue veins mapping their
decades together. Every day he visits,
waiting to see some spark of memory
in her eyes; the knowledge of his presence,

forgotten yet familiar. He holds her cold
hands, scrubbing them between his own
to warm them, and links their fingers,
stroking her knuckles with his thumb.

Reverie

Everything is as you left it.
The stack of books on your
nightstand, the photographs
lining the bureau, your shoes

lined up beneath the bed.
A crossword lies by your
place at the table, eternally
unfinished, a pencil guarding

the half-filled squares.
Your favorite mug sits empty:
Every crevice holds your spoor.
A strand of your hair still clings

to the cool whiteness of the pillow,
your scent like perfume in the air.

Prague

I walk these cobbled streets,
imagining your hand in mine,
the sunset aflame in your hair.

Every flavor, every taste falls to the bottom of me.
I am hollow inside. Without your eloquent eye,
your talent for transfiguration, I cannot feel the many lives

breathing beside me, sense the stories waiting to be told.
I cannot appreciate the the beauty of the light on the river,
the elegance of sculptured bridges and patrician trees,

these ancient walls of rain-cold stone.
Alone in my hotel suite, supine on gray silk,
emptiness beside me where your body ought to be.

I remember other beds, your silhouette in the sheets,
the light on your bare shoulders, the warmth in your eyes,
your laugh ringing in the air like church bells.

I walk along damp streets, passing monuments
and cathedrals, blind to any thoughts but you.
The city flames with color in the light of your smile.

Heirlooms

A box is a symbol, a metaphor, a noun.
It is trinket, tool, secret-keeper,
the lid worn smooth as a stone
by whispering fingertips.

The box is fragile, splintering with age,
its yellowed wood the color of a number-two pencil,
a reliquary for pressed flowers and curls of hair.
Or was the box put to a more prosaic purpose,

a receptacle for handwritten sales slips,
hairpins, heirloom brooches, or gloves with buttons
that glisten pearly as a fish's eye?
Words are knives exposed in cold air,

inked onto pages now musty with time
and the lonely hint of a lingering perfume.

Miranda

This island is all you have ever known.
Rocky beaches where waves froth
like embroidery, yet are cold as steel.
You walked barefoot and picked fruit,

climbed trees and wore cloth torn
from the sails of a shipwrecked vessel,
your feet crusted with sand.
They arrived dressed in strange doublets,

chilled and clinging to slabs of broken wood.
They stumbled ashore on shaking legs,
starved and worn from catastrophic seas.
You cannot fathom foreign lands

full of smoky cities crowded with people.
Your eyes know the cool flatness of the shore,
your ears the changing tempo of the winds.
You bend to the prickling palm bark,

whispering secrets to the leaves, to the starfish.
You practice dancing with the waves,
water sweeping your ankles like a petticoat.
You have long imagined Love.

You do not know what you were born to.
a world of courts and ladies, of rigid nobility.
Could you remember the colors of the storm,
the scent of the sea? Is that why

you cried out for the marooned sailors,
unbeknownst to you, your kin?
You have no recollection of your own tempest,
the journey a chasm in your memory.

Stardust

There are flecks of stardust in her eyes,
dark and gentle, glinting gold like mica.
The curve of her slow-spreading smile

lights her face in a candlelit glow which
leaves me breathless. The silvery laugh,
making dimples twitch in the corners of

her lips. Eyelashes flicker over delicate
cheekbones, freckles curving beneath
liquid eyes like the markings of a jaguar.

Her skin is the color of skimmed cream,
ivory stippled with gold, dappled velvet.
Her every atom delights me; the sound

of her voice warms and draws me near.
The delicate curves of neck and shoulder,
the hollow of her throat, the notches of

her clavicle make me ache with longing.
Her hair drifts against her cheek, into
moonlit eyes gleaming like hidden ore.

Desire

Overwhelmed by intensity, the senses
cannot concentrate. My fingers strain
to touch him, playing invisible music
in the air. I long to soak in the atoms

of his scent, to absorb him through
every pore. Without the comfort of his
presence, the air feels thinner, and my
muscles tense. When he returns, the

world seems easier to manage. My lips
seek the warm pulp of his mouth,
probing every crevice of tooth and tongue.
I scrub my cheek into the hollow of his

shoulder like a satisfied cat, grazing the
fabric of his coat as I nestle there, a perfect fit.

Another Storm

I feel the rising storm with preternatural clarity,
hear the drumroll of thunder in my inner ear.
Panic prickles through my veins and along my spine

in a full-body spasm, as involuntary and uncontrollable
as a seizure, an invisible tremor, painful in its intensity:
an electrical storm of the mind, a frisson of fear making

the ice rattle in my glass, the book tremble in my hand.
The explosion starts in my chest and bursts along my
limbs, making them stiffen and shudder. I can feel the

thump and throb of my pulse in every joint and muscle.
The lion's roar of thunder spurs my rabbit-rapid heartbeat
as beacons of lightning flash overhead like fierce tempers.

My body creates a catastrophe where there is none.
My limbs are bird-boned, empty and hollow, my aspic
legs rubbery with anxiety. I am a cat with rippled fur,

whiskers prickling with prescience, pulse trembling.
I feel each thud and tremor of the cosmic conniption
in the pained hummingbird flutter of my leaping heart.

Nerves

My body vibrates with expectancy.
Every muscle, every tendon burns
from this self-administered shock treatment,
tension pulsing like the colors of flashing neon signs,

pain radiating red, blue, and green in my mind's eye.
The blooming synapse sparks and spreads,
igniting spiderwebs of dendrites. Thought-pollen
flies from one mind-flower to another.

My galvanized nerve endings itch and hum.
They tremble in the searing shock of spasm,
red with heat instead of hemoglobin,
as though boiling water runs in my veins.

The lit fuse of my burning nerves stings with every step,
the bone-deep throb of joints panicked and inflamed.

Images

I am a treasure hunter,
eager as a wildcat silently stalking prey.
Captivated by texture and those precise accidents

known as serendipity, my subconscious
links details into patterns, finding synchronicity.
The human eye is clouded, overstimulated by detail.

The black box of the camera parses the scene,
sweeping away the nimbus obscuring the view,
deepening the revelations caught by the mirror

of its eye. I thrive on these discoveries, the explosion
as a thought breaks the surface of the complex
rivers of neurons and joyfully catches the light.

Spirituality

A large bleached Buddha crouches on the altar,
a low table strewn with spiritual paraphernalia,
the tools of a witch: incense, mortar and pestle,
candles, crystal spikes of amethyst and quartz.

True spirituality lies in creativity.
The superstitions of the theatre are no stranger,
no less powerful, than the rites of a priest.
With scripts instead of spellbooks

we worship at the altar of the proscenium.
The thick red gourd lamps light our faces
as we wait for the ritual to begin.
We intone our lines like shamans casting cantrips,

listening to the colors of our voices with every breath.
We fill the hollow shells of our bodies
with other personas, multiple personalities,
in a subconscious altered state.

Backstage

Costumes glitter like the plumage of tropical birds,
skirts winking sequins, frothing whitecaps of tulle.
Colorful gowns seem to glow in eager anticipation,
as if they know they are about to make their debut.

Hats perch like birds' nests along dusty eaves,
wooden wig heads staring as blindly as Sibyls.
Swaddled in the bat-wings of black curtains,
as industrious as ants as we sort and arrange,

outfitting make-believe lives.
Within the microcosm of stage and set,
an ethereal creature is born.
Like an insect it lives for a single night,

shimmering, ephemeral, only to die when
the solar system of spotlights are dimmed.

Rehearsal

Threading along the dark recesses of the theatre,
through the rabbit-warren of wings, stands a backstage
tableau of stacked chairs and scattered props,
the black skirt of the curtain drawn like a sail unfurling.

A scrim of sawdust felts the flats; folded ladders
lean and slouch. Dark knots burn like sightless eyes
in the wood, unpainted and splintering. People skulk
and scurry backstage, as darkly-clad as cat burglars;

specters presiding over a rummage-sale hodgepodge
of objects, assembling and rearranging worlds with
every scene. Actors stand poised in the wings, straining
for cues. They grin with fierce hilarity, struggling to remain

silent with all the desperate necessity of Anne Frank hiding
in the attic, struggling to engender microcosmic lives,
tasting the flavors of the words on their tongues,
savoring the precision of a perfect phrase.

Blue Rhapsody

A flicker of the keys, a rising skirl.
Notes unfold like flowers:
The clarinet trills a glissando,

a sweet twisting strain.
The horn rolls like a woman's hips,
like running water, fresh and blue.

Chords twinkle in the air like stardust.
Fingers scuttle like crabs over the keys,
meeting the joyful trumpet's lazy drawl.

Violinists cradle the polished curves
of their instruments like swaddled infants,
a melody like the breath of sleeping children.

Silent Sentinels

Brave banners are wind-dashed and mud-stained;
hat plumes hang sodden. They do not feel the sleet,
only the iron of their convictions. Courtly gentlemen

spit at the women to whom they once bowed.
Insolent women, in classrooms, on picket lines,
in settlement houses, handcuffed to iron gates.

Clad in sashes like knights marching into battle;
their embroidered armor bearing the strident statements
of equality. Insolent women, refusing to be chattel!

Ode to Katharine Hepburn

A thoroughbred Artemis,
statuesque and Puritanical
in your uniform of white shirt
and khakis, a pale taper lit by

a Titian topknot of flaming curls.
Taurean stubbornness runs along
veins of Main Line steel, headstrong
Yankee indomitability even sharper

than your bone structure,
those stark architectural cheekbones.
Your hair is a wiry thatch of copper,
a mare's mane flowing as you run,

a force of nature as freckled as a tiger lily,
diving undaunted into the wintry Atlantic.

Cat Eyes

In darkened doorways
she ambles, gold-glowing eyes
gleaming like the moon.

The Crimson Rug

I

A vivid kilim
blazes underfoot, starkly
stippled with Morse code:

II

The spotted snake of
dominoes winding its way
across the expanse.

Madonna and Child

Full-lipped Madonnas hold swaddled babies,
their cloths mingling with the dewlaps of dark
mantles. Sloe-eyed and olive-skinned, their

gazes held by the fat golden cherubs in their
arms. The devout look of the mother, sure of
the purity and charm of her innocent child.

She is a Persephone, aubergine stains of sorrow
beneath her eyes, a pensive and downcast gaze,
her long, elegant fingers plucking at her face in

anguished penance. Clad in a hair-shirt of guilt,
mourning the brutal undoing of her gentle son.
Five hundred years later, her pain still radiates.

If she had stood here in this gallery, gazing into
the eyes of stoic, patient mothers and rosy infants,
she might have achieved a sense of closure from

the pain of her lost child. She did not know that
his courage and kindness would be immortalized
by painters. She knew only suffering and love.

Painting Mary Magdalene

Her mantle is brown, the tawny chestnut
of a fawn's hide. Twin curves of shoulder,
neck and bosom bared, her linen chemise
a serene bluish-grey, as delicate as a dove.

Carmine, madder, vermilion and cinnabar:
Poisonous ores the color of Christ's blood.
the longest wavelength in the human eye.
Five centuries have not dulled the golden

patina of vestments rendered in the yellow
spices of saffron, gamboge, orpiment, ochre.
Five hundred years later, pain still radiates
in unrelenting waves, her face as white as

bone smeared on canvas. She kneels at the
feet of umber-clad priests, aching for solace.

Bruegel's Bride

(Pieter Bruegel the Elder, "Peasant Wedding", 1569)

Robust, ruddy-cheeked peasants
swarthy with ale clap the rhythm
of a ring-dance to the birdsong of
the drunken piper. A wedding feast,

gorging on trestles laden with fowl
from peacock to partridge, piecrust
and crisp loaves like the sunburnt
breasts of fishwives and wenches.

The mythological cupbearer pours
waterfalls of beer into waiting steins,
raised in a hearty toast, and refilled.
Freckled fishwives with storybook

faces whisper about the wedding night,
lappets flapping, stays taut with bloating.
The bride is pale beneath a paper crown,
her nuptial wreath as fragile as her status.

Tomorrow she will become a beast of burden,
a brood mare, a pack mule, a teat-swollen sow.
In the barn of piled straw and weathered wood
the dun-colored monk begins the wedding vows.

Mona Lisa

A Mediterranean face, muted and mellow,
the color of a Tuscan sunset.
Countless lovers have stared into your slanted eyes,
serene as Mary Magdalene.

Broad peasant shoulders are clad in linen
the color of furrowed fields,
withered and chapped with wrinkles,
weathered and cracked like broken pottery.

You are ancient as an oak, yet somehow ageless,
an enigma, your lips tilted in a delicate cat's smile.
The salt of the earth, ripe and maternal,
somehow patrician and proletariat at once.

Your canvas is weighted with five centuries
of secrets hidden behind espresso-dark eyes.

Posing for Renoir

(Pierre-Auguste Renoir, "Dance at Bougival", 1883)

The dress is a waterfall of ruffles,
filmy layers embroidered with the
white shadows of flowers. Lace inserts
within chiffon, like winter windowpanes

etched with ice, the sheer mesh as fragile
as a dragonfly's wing. Beneath my skirt,
petticoats foam like the sea; silk stockings
whispering against my legs while we waltz.

Casa Azul

An Ode to Frida Kahlo

The table is cluttered with bottles and tubes
squeezed and rolled like toothpaste, their tips
clotted and scabbed with dried paint. Here the
consummation of tint and hue are performed,

the yin and yang of colors: Red dips to blue,
begetting purple. Red is diluted to pink on the
advice of white, and meets yellow in secret,
their affair siring sunset. The huge old canopy

bed, the convalescent's chamber, lies among
carnival-colored statues and painted furniture.
Here you lay stranded, a plaster golem, pained
and restless inside the concrete carapace that

binds your broken vertebrae. Bedridden, you lay
on embroidered pillows, spending endless hours
contemplating the ceiling, decorating yourself with
rings on every finger, and floral garlands in your hair.

Greenwich Village

For Diane di Prima

We lounge on the floor like contented pets,
drinking green tea from painted stoneware.
Colorful drifts of silk and faded paisley
cover the old worn chaise where we lie

together in a serene orgy, your long red hair
fanned on the pillows like flames. Our tangled
bodies leave imprints like snow angels in the sheets
as candles flicker and reflect in the night-dark glass.

Along the Amazon

Dense trees draped with rope-thick vines
winding among green boughs, concealing
the snakes that lie within, hidden against
mossy bark the texture of crocodile hides.

Colors here are an amazement of riches:
parrots striped and streaked like sunsets,
the gradient rainbow of the scarlet macaw,
and sudden flashes of passing butterflies.

Tousled lilies and vivid flowers I cannot name,
the rosy lips of the hibiscus blossom, lushly red.
Even the trees seem to sweat in this humid swamp,
of a green too bright and strange to be believed.

A toucan stares with his bright cocked head,
his banded banana-beak weighing him down.
The heavy heads of flytraps nod,
their spiky maws tasting the air.

Through the fronds burns the steady obsidian gaze
of the prowling jaguar, elegant and intense, mottled
gold. Shrieks and screeches of marmosets ring out,
their amusingly ugly faces invisible among the boughs.

Green Shadows

I

The fascinating
patterns of bark, textures of
roots and mottled leaves.

II

Mysterious green
knotholes, columns weeping moss,
verdant woods glowing.

III

Ivy-clad among
green-headed ghosts of branches,
endless shades of green.

Waltz of the Hawks

Elegant hawks fan against the blue-swirled sky,
the serene grace of their white-tipped wings
whirling against a backdrop streaked with clouds.

The knight's hawk circles overhead,
surveying the landscape with a shrewd
gemstone-yellow eye. She is a predator,

narrow and elegant as a blade,
all beak and shining talons.
Skimming the ground like a river stone,

flashing scimitars snap at panicked prey,
dangling limply from the claws of the hunt goddess
soaring overhead, her triumphant shriek like a cold wind.

Wetlands

A white egret sits
along the curve of the pond,
drinking its blue sheen.

Landscape

I

Feathery cattails,
their greenness bisected by
a precise white fence.

II

Cornsilk-pale, dancing
to the rhythm of the wind,
green breezes blowing.

The Gathering Storm

Clouds lie in furrows
like a plowed field, white rows stacked
to the horizon.

Reconstruction

Tangled skeins of kudzu drape their green circus
tents over shtetl-shacks and tilting fences, winding
like ivy through wooden slats into the pores of the

swollen, rain-soaked boards. Precarious stacks of
crumbling bricks, rust, worn wood, peeling paint,
scabrous stucco, copper vases patina-ed with age,

their mouths greening with ringworms of tarnish.
The exposed floors are dusty and canted, listing
like vertigo. Wallpaper curls like a cresting wave,

streaked with tears, studded with the blinded eyes
of corroded mirrors. The whole effect is of decay,
something moldering and warping in the humid air.

Fallen Leaves

The maple tree ages gracefully,
growing lighter with each leaf
wrenched by the autumn breeze.
Her branches shake with mirth,

a joy she feels down to her roots.
She is serene with the coming of
winter, unafraid of melodramatic
winds. Songbirds are drawn to her

russet radiance, the patience of
the sovereign tree. Her wisdom
is carried on the wind, whispered
by every rustling branch, written

on falling leaves glinting with colors soon faded,
their hidden messages scrawled in invisible ink.

Death in Autumn

The leaves drift like sibyls, outstretched hands
floating on the wind, eager to taste the air.
Parched and asthmatic, tightening protectively
as clenched fists, sere veins drying to papery crispness.
They accept their deaths bravely, drifting to sleep

on sidewalks like doorstep drunkards. They feel the pulse
of autumn in each creaking branch and scrap of bark
pulled by the wind. They feel the voice of time deep in their
tap roots, riding the wind, drifting like feathers,
like flower petals, rasping underfoot like the hiss of a flame.

Sacred Trees

Yew trees whisper
to the wafting smoke,
their secrets drifting
like spice-scented steam
from the yellow map of veins
on each old and storied leaf.

The Guise of the Phoenix

For five thousand years he hibernates, a feathery sage
musing the mysteries of the universe, his nest of acacia
twigs wafting spices through the air. With a flick of a
wing, he ignites in a pyrotechnic display. He is a spy,

a secret agent, a classified document self-destructing
in the flames. He will spontaneously combust after
revealing a single golden secret. His mind contains
the wisdom of the ages, a library of ancient gilded

volumes in many different languages. He is known
by many names, exchanging alter egos as easily as
molting singed plumage. Rumors surround him,
swirling like smoke in the air. Some say it was the

Phoenix who aided God in making Lazarus rise from
the dead, transplanting his tears for the resurrection.

Between Pacific Tides

Far out to sea, rakish sea lions converse
with St. Francis beneath the steely scrim
of Pacific fog. Their barking can be heard,
tenor notes against the baritone of foghorns.
Pastel periwinkles and stippled star-shaped
pincushions are startled awake at the sound,
lying supine along the craggy plateau of rock.

Tarpon River, Fort Lauderdale

Manatees dwell in the slow brown river,
submarine shadows like cataracts
floating through the palm-shaded depths.
Their gray girth swells and spreads
as they pass beneath the rippling tide.

Northern Lights

The pack ice resembles a mosaic of broken tiles where pups croak and croon, rolling playfully, enjoying the sensation of snow. Mothers plump and banded nurse pups who expand balloon-like as their fur gradually

darkens: ice-white, butter-blond, and dappled silver. They swirl in greenish water, trailing auras of bubbles behind them in a serpentine interpretive dance, joyful, reveling in their element. The silent fireworks of the

aurora borealis flash overhead like searchlights, mint, mauve, cobalt, barium green and methane blue, glowing while above them, polar bears stalk the icy plateau like wardens, waiting, tints glinting in their colorless fur.

Evil Stars

The heavenly darkling waits with cruel patience,
the green Eden-snake of its vine uncurling with
feral intent. It savors the moment when the scab
bursts like an aneurism, leaving destruction in

its wake: the tumbled population of war vets, of
collapsed fronts, of communal suicides. Hydrogen,
that apocalyptic fuse, strikes like a mythic Fury.
The white dwarf, like those harboring the spore of

its starlit succubus, lives intensely, and evaporates
with a quicksilver brevity. Lithium is high-strung
and flammable, fed to the manic, the frenzied; the
birds beating at their cages. These elements, when

aged, create a star with the potential for greatness,
if only from the magnitude of its own destruction.

Runestones

The words ring inside me,
reverberating off my ribcage,
bouncing between bones.

They burn on my tongue,
each one a different color.
Peel them out of my skull,

bleed them from my fingertips,
syllable by syllable, like rain.
I soak in language like a warm bath,

bursting from the water, soaking the pages
with my thoughts. Stories wind their way
through my bloodstream, cell by cell.

Seized from the marrow of my bones,
they burn across the page like wildfire,
unearthed letter by letter, like sand-scoured runes.

Memories breathe, setting my senses alight.
My skin is streaked with my past lives, their
music swelling my flesh, ripe as bursting fruit.

Words

The tyranny of the blank page,
mockingly white, like the frustration
of my barren mind, seeking rich,
rambling words, metaphors with

plenty of meat on the bone. I gather
synonyms to strew, berry-picking
phrases like a pearl diver among
the oyster beds, counting every

syllable, seeking precision, tasting
the flavors of distant languages
as I struggle toward plausible rhymes.
I am a surgeon, suturing phrases

in neat rows like stitches, transferring
images from the mind's eye.
The epidermis of the page unfolds,
revealing the dermatology of punctuation:

the ellipsis of freckles, fat moles
like consonants, mouths bracketed
by parentheses. The challenge is to
transcribe the muse, pen poised like

an arrow aimed at pinstriped pages,
catching every word, staring down
the hostile emptiness of a sheaf of
blank pages waiting to be filled.

Irises

Golden-throated, streaked
with sunlight, petals curving
like a waving hand.

Spring Rain

The promise of rain:
Undaunted by the cold air,
birds sing nonetheless.

Words and Music

Rain drums the windowpanes like percussion
as the storm crescendoes, the glass streaming.
Such a day calls for jazz. Ella's tongue-twisting
scat reminds me of the precision of language,

experiments with sound, rhythm and syllable.
I tap my pencil in time to her crooning strain,
pondering "Lionel Hampton's instrument": ten
letters, starts with V. My pencil stutters against

the tabletop, keeping time as I count the spaces,
testing each letter to see whether the potential
combination makes a word. With each completed
clue, another cross-street appears on the grid,

the black and white squares as stark as sheet music.
The last note hangs in the air; the last blank white
space waits to be filled, a single vowel making the
difference between gibberish and a genuine word.

The Front Page

The typist's practiced hand tightens
a new sheet of blank paper into place.
The rhythmic drumbeat of pounding
fingers resembles the factory roar of

clattering gears and rushing motors.
The bell chimes, a single sedate note
amidst the cacophony, then the rasp
of the carriage being pushed back to

a fresh margin. The filled page is torn
and stacked among the white flags of
piled papers on a desktop strewn with
scattered sheets and broken pencils.

Skin

Blue tributaries
of veins spread from the milky
whiteness of my wrist.

Summer Fruit

Textures and similes abound as we select summer fruit,
squeezing the juicy red hefts of tomatoes, solid and round;
velvety apricots, lemons like handfuls of sunshine, and

the pocked red hearts of strawberries. Mottled apples
and pale, mealy crescents of banana, their leathery skins
like speckled snakes. Sweet golden moons of peaches and

sunset orbs of nectarines mingle in the bowl, waiting to
be consumed. The sweetness of their scent is heady, rich;
syrupy juice dripping summery stickiness. Blood oranges

resemble miniature suns, bright paper lanterns strung
for a garden party. Bruise-colored plums, bitten and bloody,
fruit peels like citrus-scented leather, the crunch of grapes,

and spongy bowls of grapefruit with hearts of rosy pulp.
The great boulder of the watermelon awaits its execution,
its green beetle-shell striped like malachite. Cleaved open,

it will reveal its damp center like a geode, darkly studded
with seeds, to be devoured by tongues streaked violet by
freshly-picked blueberries, fingers blood-stained by juice.

Tahitian Landscape

The incandescent fever dream of Gauguin, a landscape as vivid
as Rousseau's jungle, its foliage lush as tropical fruit.
Citrus shades of sunset abound even in the heat of the day,

burning with malarial intensity in the sweating tropical air:
Cerise, chartreuse, persimmon, nectarine, mango, and peach.
Sweat gleams on languid bronze bodies, running like the juice

from freshly-picked fruit, papaya breasts bared above
knotted pareos. Blossoms burn against dark hair, lank
as bay-mare manes: sunset, salmon, azalea, flamingo, coral,

orange, orchid, lavender. Intense colors suit their strong
carved faces, cocoa complexions of coffee, ochre, umber,
stark cheekbones glinting gold against the searing sun.

Potatoes

Potatoes tumble from burlap sacks,
heaped like speckled stones, laying
damp and cool in my hand, their heft
weighed in the paleness of my palm.

Ancient skin is scratched and scarred,
punctuated with moles and liver spots.
The peeler scrapes away the epidermis
of coarse brown paper, revealing gold,

like ore damply shaken from a miner's pan.
The glint of wielded steel, deftly separating
the toad-like complexion from the prize within.
The brown rind peels away like curling ribbon,

exposing yellow flesh punctured by thumbprints.
The wet-grass scent of freshly-shaven potatoes
bobbing in a bowl like a children's game, watery
submersibles left to float like seals in a rookery.

The piled parings resemble rhinoceros hides:
The satisfaction of mounding vegetable peels
heaped like pine straw, the pile of potato skin
strewn like gift wrap on Christmas morning.

The methodical scrape of the peeler as it shreds
the brown tree-bark roughness like scaling fish.
Metaphors abound, similes curling into the air
above as the potatoes slowly fill the empty bowl.

Soul Song

I am afraid of love, of the potential for pain
that lies hidden beneath the underbelly.
I instinctively turn away, betraying
my own chance for safety, for kindness.

I so badly need the tenderness
you're offering, but I do not possess
the easy grace to reciprocate.
My well of safety must be filled.

Is it better to be alone and sure of myself,
tightening my circumstances into something
I can control, or believe I can,
or to throw caution to the wind,

recklessly, with open arms,
and embrace life in all its uncertainty?

About the Author

A fifth-generation New Yorker, Jessica Goody was born and raised on Long Island. She currently lives in the South Carolina Lowcountry with an exuberant poodle named Coco.

Her debut poetry collection *Defense Mechanisms: Poems on Life, Love, and Loss* was released by Phosphene Publishing in 2016 and is available from Amazon in Kindle and paperback.

Jessica is a columnist for *SunSations Magazine*. Her writing has appeared in over three dozen publications, including *The Wallace Stevens Journal*, *Chicken Soup for the Soul*, *Reader's Digest*, and *The Maine Review*. Her work has been nominated for numerous awards, winning the 2016 *Magnets and Ladders* Poetry Prize.

Made in the USA
Columbia, SC
10 March 2019